D0742470

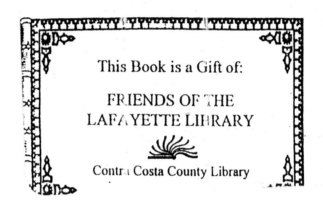

Nocturnal Animals

Fennec Foxes

Kristin Petrie
ABDO Publishing Company

visit us at
www.abdopublishing.com

Published by ABDO Publishing Company, 8000 West 78th Street, Edina, Minnesota 55439.
Copyright © 2010 by Abdo Consulting Group, Inc. International copyrights reserved in all
countries. No part of this book may be reproduced in any form without written permission from the
publisher. The Checkerboard Library™ is a trademark and logo of ABDO Publishing Company.

Printed in the United States of America, North Mankato, Minnesota.
082009
012010

 PRINTED ON RECYCLED PAPER

Cover Photo: Alamy
Interior Photos: Alamy pp. 6, 17; Animals Animals pp. 5, 8; Corbis p. 18;
    Getty Images pp. 10, 13, 21; Peter Arnold pp. 12, 15, 16; Photo Researchers p. 1;
    Public Domain p. 7

Series Coordinator: Megan M. Gunderson
Editors: Megan M. Gunderson, BreAnn Rumsch
Art Direction & Cover Design: Neil Klinepier

Library of Congress Cataloging-in-Publication Data

Petrie, Kristin, 1970-
  Fennec foxes / Kristin Petrie.
       p. cm. -- (Nocturnal animals)
  Includes index.
  ISBN 978-1-60453-736-9
  1. Fennec--Juvenile literature. I. Title.
  QL737.C22P476 2010
  599.776--dc22
                                2009025653

Contents

Fennec Foxes

What creature lives in the desert, has huge ears, and walks on furry feet? It rarely drinks water, and it stays up all night. No, it's not a camel or even a teenager! This special animal is the fennec fox.

The fennec fox is best known for its oversize ears. It is a nocturnal mammal from the order Carnivora. Animals in this order are mainly meat eaters. However, some carnivores such as the fennec fox also eat plants. This makes them omnivores.

Twelve families make up the order Carnivora. The fennec fox is a member of the family **Canidae**. Dogs, wolves, jackals, and other foxes are also canids.

Nocturnal, Diurnal, or Crepuscular?

One way scientists group animals is by when they are most active. Nocturnal animals work and play during the night and sleep during the day. Diurnal animals are the opposite. They rest at night and are active during the day. Crepuscular animals are most active at twilight. This includes the time just before sunrise or just after sunset.

The fennec and several other foxes belong to the genus *Vulpes*. *Vulpes* is Latin for "fox." The fennec fox's species name is *zerda*, which is Greek for "cunning." *Vulpes zerda* is the perfect name for this tiny, clever creature!

Scientists use a method called scientific classification to sort organisms into groups. The basic classification system includes eight groups. In descending order, they are domain, kingdom, phylum, class, order, family, genus, and species.

Ears to Tail

What if your ears were one-third as long as your body? At five feet (1.5 m) tall, your ears would be 20 inches (51 cm) long!

The fennec fox is the smallest member of the family **Canidae**. Fully grown, a fennec only weighs about 3.3 pounds (1.5 kg). It is 8 inches (20 cm) tall from paw to shoulder. A fennec's total head and body length is between 14 and 16 inches (36 and 41 cm). Its bushy tail adds another 7 to 12 inches (18 to 31 cm).

Amazingly, the fennec fox's ears can be more than six inches (15 cm) long. That makes them about one-third as long as its body!

The fur on a fennec's feet can be up to one-half inch (1.3 cm) long.

A coat of long, thick, sandy-colored fur covers the fennec's body. This reflects daytime heat and **insulates** the animal from cold desert nights. Equally important, it provides camouflage.

A fennec fox's legs vary in color. Depending on the animal's **habitat**, they may be a reddish sand color or nearly white. Darker fur extends from the large eyes down either side of the **muzzle**. The tip and base of the tail are black. The ears are dark on the back and nearly white inside.

The fennec's feet are another special feature. Fur covers the soles. This protects the feet from hot sand. And, it helps the fennec walk on loose sand.

Desert Home

To see a fennec fox in nature, you would need to travel to Africa. The fennec roams Africa's northern desert regions. Its range is large. The fennec fox can be found from Tunisia to Chad and from Mauritania to Egypt.

As many as ten fennec foxes may live together in one burrow.

The fennec fox spends most of the day in its underground burrow, or den. In softer sand, a fennec fox den may be small and have just one entrance. Desert grasses and other plants line and strengthen the den.

In compact soil, a den may be larger. It can have as many as 15 entrances. These holes lead to one burrow or a network of burrows. Large burrows may cover 1,300 square feet (120 sq m) of land!

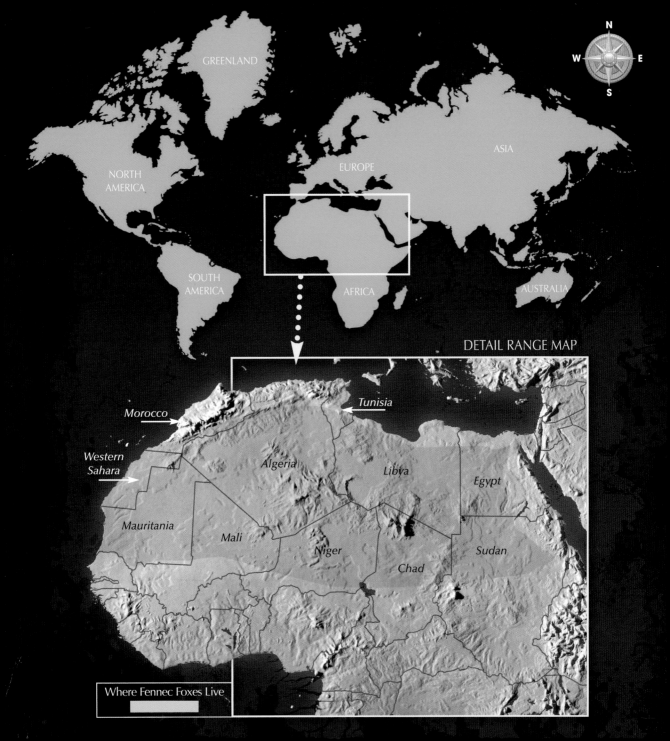

N
W — E
S

GREENLAND

NORTH
AMERICA

EUROPE

ASIA

SOUTH
AMERICA

AFRICA

AUSTRALIA

DETAIL RANGE MAP

Morocco

Tunisia

*Western
Sahara*

Algeria

Libya

Egypt

Mauritania

Mali

Niger

Chad

Sudan

Where Fennec Foxes Live

Active at Night

Now you have found a fennec fox burrow entrance. But you must wait until dark to see a fennec. The fennec fox spends the hot daytime hours resting in its underground burrow. This nocturnal fox stays up during the night instead!

Having good night vision allows the fennec to avoid hunting during hot desert days.

The fennec fox is also known for crepuscular activity. In Morocco's cooler winter weather, it may be active as late as midmorning.

The fennec fox is well suited to its nocturnal habits. Its large eyes help give it great night vision. And, its large ears provide great hearing in the desert. These senses help it find prey and avoid predators.

Some lucky nocturnal animals have special eye features that help them in the dark. They may have large eyes compared to their body size. Also, their pupils may open wider than ours do in low light. These two features allow more light to enter their eyes.

After light enters an eye's pupil, the lens focuses it on the retina. In the retina, two special kinds of cells receive the light. These are rods and cones.

Rods work in low light. They detect size, shape, and brightness. Cones work in bright light. They detect color and details. Nocturnal animals often have many more rods than cones.

Many nocturnal eyes also have a tapetum lucidum behind the retina. The tapetum is like a mirror. Light bounces off of it and back through the retina a second time. This gives the light another chance to strike the rods. The reflected light then continues back out through the pupil. This causes the glowing eyes you may see at night!

RODS

CONES

RETINA

RETINA

TAPETUM LUCIDUM

RETINA →

LENS —

PUPIL

ANIMAL'S EYE (side view)

Digging for Food

As omnivores, fennec foxes happily feast on animals and plants. They are also opportunistic feeders. This means they eat whatever food is available. Fennec foxes are known to store food for later, too.

Fennec foxes may live in groups, but they hunt alone. Their oversize ears help them locate prey moving under the sand. Then, they quickly dig it up!

Fennec foxes have several favorite foods, including insects and small **rodents**. Lizards, geckos, eggs, and small birds also make a tasty meal. Fennec foxes eat fruits and **tubers** as well.

Food provides fennecs with the small amount of water they need to survive. They also have water-saving **kidneys**. Fennecs can live in the desert without a sip to drink! Yet if water is available, they will drink it.

The fennec fox eats tiny rodents, such as the jerboa.

To save food for later, a fennec fox digs a hole and deposits the food. Then, it uses its nose to push sand over the food.

Young Fennecs

The fennec fox's life starts after a male and a female mate. Scientists believe fennecs mate once per year, usually in January or February.

The female fennec fox carries two to five young at a time. They are born 51 days after mating. The young are tiny, furry, blind, and helpless at birth. Mothers care for their young. Fathers provide food for the mothers and defend the burrow.

The young first open their eyes after 8 to 11 days. At four weeks, they begin to play inside the den. Around five weeks, the young begin leaving the den. However, they stay very close to it. Fennecs become independent around six months of age. Yet, they may remain with their families.

It is not known how long the fennec fox lives in the wild. In **captivity**, females have lived for 13 years. Males have lived for 14 years.

Having more than one litter in a single year is unusual for canids.
Yet if the first litter dies, fennec foxes may have a second.

Desert Dangers

Striped hyenas

What can affect how long the fennec fox lives? Natural predators! The eagle owl preys on fennec fox young. The jackal and the striped hyena may also attack the fennec fox. Some people have even reported **domestic** dogs preying on the fennec.

Luckily, the fennec fox is considered very difficult to catch. Its large ears help it detect and avoid its enemies. And, the fennec's sandy-colored fur helps it blend into its **habitat**.

While running, the fennec fox can change direction quickly. Burrow openings offer a quick escape from enemies. The fennec can also dig a new hole with great speed. This little fox is an impressive jumper, too. It can jump 24 inches (60 cm) high and 47 inches (120 cm) straight out!

The fennec fox's fur acts as camouflage to help protect it from enemies.

Humans are the fennec fox's number one enemy. The fennec fox is difficult to spot in the wild. So, humans trap the small fox alive. These animals are then shown to tourists or sold as pets. In some areas, people trap the fennec fox for its meat and fur.

Taking fennec foxes from the wild threatens their ecosystem. Fennecs help control **rodent**, locust, and other pest populations. Yet today, many fennec foxes are killed or captured. This could leave too many pests, which can then harm crops.

The fennec fox also faces **habitat** loss. For example, the fennec fox population disappeared from several areas in southern Morocco. These areas were near new human settlements.

In addition, the fennec fox faces challenges from the desert itself. Fennec fox **litters** are smaller than those of other foxes. This slow reproduction rate may be due to their harsh habitat. The fennec fox faces hot sun and sand, few plants, and little water. Yet it is well adapted to these challenges. Its furry paws, large ears, and nocturnal habits help it survive.

Some people keep fennec foxes as pets. However, it is illegal to own them in some areas of the United States.

The Future of Fennecs

Scientists do not have enough information to determine the total fennec fox population. However, they believe the population is sufficient for now. That is because so many fennecs are available for trapping and selling.

Still, the fennec fox remains at risk of becoming **endangered**. International trade must be carefully regulated to protect its population.

Fennec fox populations already occur in protected areas in several nations. These include Algeria, Egypt, Mauritania, Niger, Tunisia, and Libya. There, national parks and **conservation** areas protect fennecs. In addition, fennecs are legally protected throughout nations such as Morocco and Western Sahara.

Scientists are learning much from fennecs in **captivity**. In the future, they hope to learn more about fennecs in the wild. If protected in their natural **habitat**, these tiny foxes will continue to thrive!

Conservation groups aim to help people study the fennec fox's role in its ecosystem. This information will demonstrate the fennec's value and what protection it needs.

Glossary

Canidae (KAN-uh-dee) - the scientific Latin name for the dog family. Members of this family are called canids. They include domestic dogs, wolves, jackals, foxes, and coyotes.

captivity - the state of being captured and held against one's will.

conservation - the planned management of natural resources to protect them from damage or destruction.

domestic - tame, especially relating to animals.

endangered - in danger of becoming extinct.

habitat - a place where a living thing is naturally found.

insulate - to keep something from losing heat.

kidney - one of a pair of organs that help the body get rid of waste products.

litter - all of the young born at one time to a mother fennec fox.

muzzle - an animal's nose and jaws.

rodent - any of several related animals that have large front teeth for gnawing. Common rodents include mice, squirrels, and beavers.

tuber - an enlarged, underground stem of a plant. A potato is a tuber.

Web Sites

To learn more about fennec foxes, visit ABDO Publishing Company on the World Wide Web at **www.abdopublishing.com**. Web sites about fennec foxes are featured on our Book Links page. These links are routinely monitored and updated to provide the most current information available.

Index